Contents

I am a nurse

My name is Kate. I am a nurse.

This is the hospital where I work.
It is called The County Hospital
and is in Hereford.

I am a children's nurse. There are twenty beds on the children's ward, and we usually have about ten **patients** at any one time.

The children's ward

Today I am on a day **shift**. I let myself in to the Children's Ward.

I put on my nurse's shirt and trousers and a badge with my name on it.

The night shift team will be going home soon. I have a quick meeting with them and Clare gives me the hand-over reports. These tell me which children are on the ward, and who will be joining us today.

Breakfast

This is Charlotte. She has just found out she has **diabetes**. She will be in the hospital for the day while the doctors do some tests.

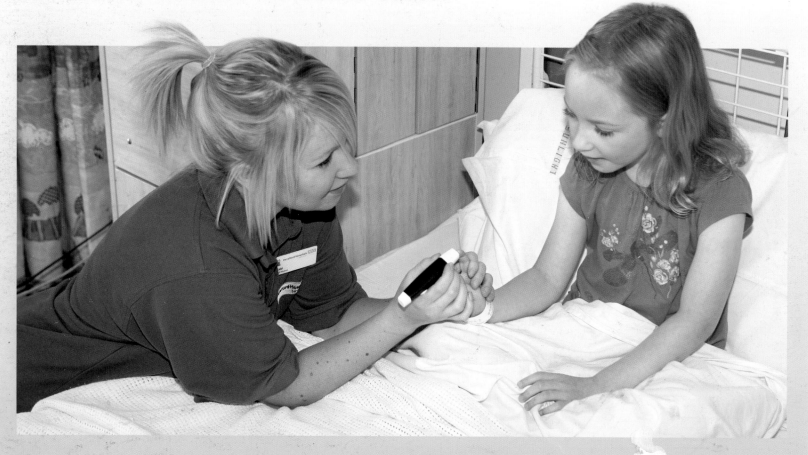

Charlotte needs a blood test. I take a tiny drop of blood with a special needle. It will be tested to see what her blood **glucose** level is.

I give Charlotte her breakfast and ask her what she would like for lunch.

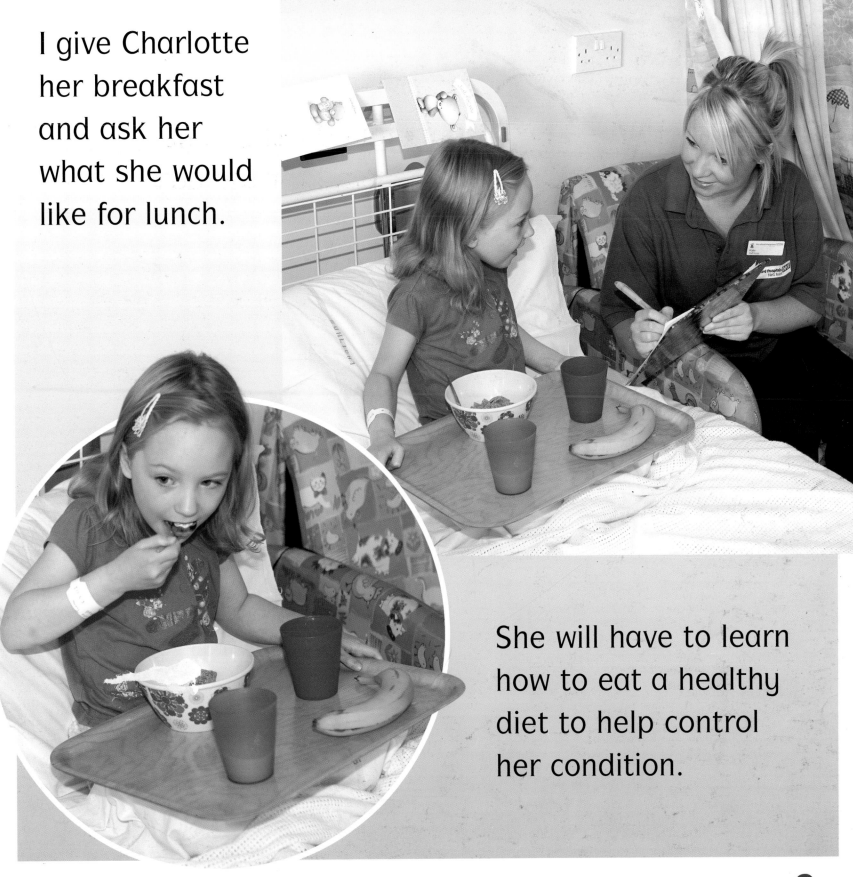

She will have to learn how to eat a healthy diet to help control her condition.

A new patient

Madeleine has arrived on the ward. Her dad has brought her in. She keeps getting **tonsillitis** and needs an operation to have her **tonsils** out.

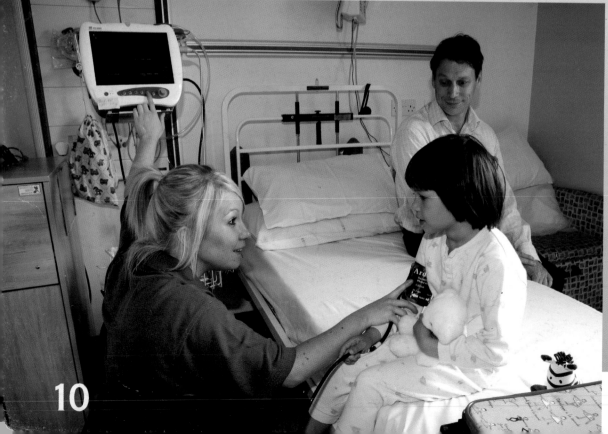

She puts her pyjamas on, and I take her **blood pressure**.

Then I weigh her on this weighing chair.
She weighs 18kg.

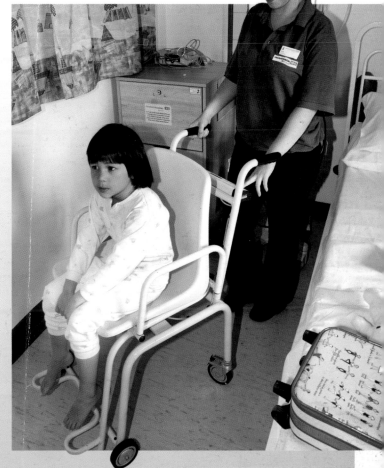

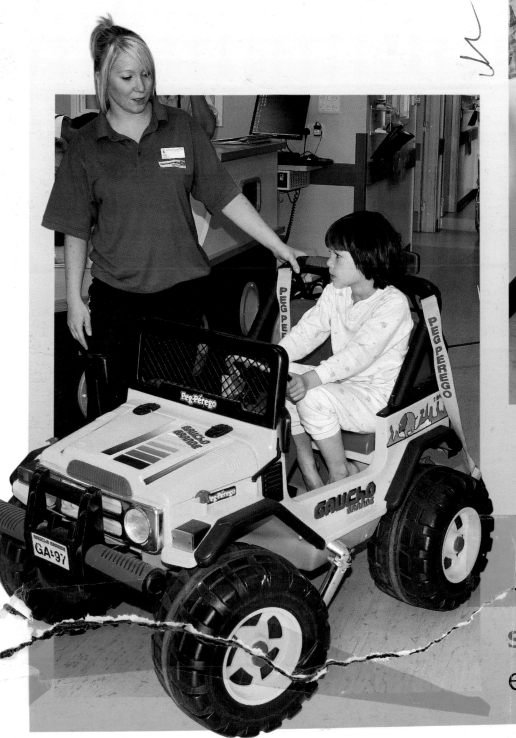

We have a special electric car for children who are going down to the theatre for surgery. Madeleine enjoys driving the car.

Ward round

Doctor Saleem has arrived to do the **ward round**.
He will check up on all the children in the ward.

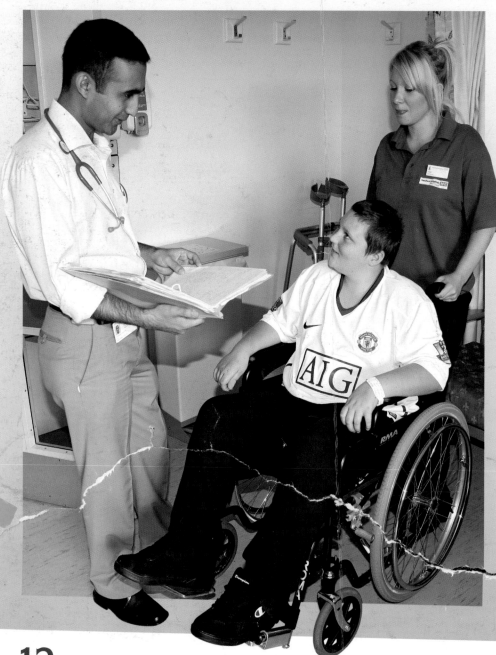

Matthew broke his legs in a car accident. Doctor Saleem looks at Matthew's notes and asks how he is feeling. Matthew will need some **physiotherapy** to help his legs get strong again.

Then the doctor sees Charlotte. He shows her an **insulin pen**. She will have to carry one around with her. The **insulin** will control her diabetes.

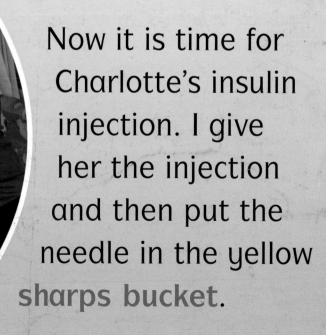

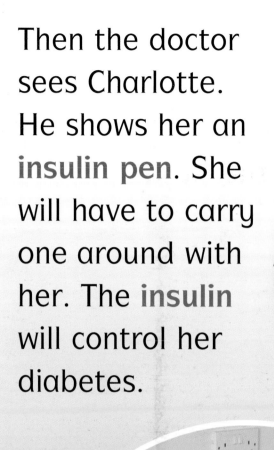

Now it is time for Charlotte's insulin injection. I give her the injection and then put the needle in the yellow **sharps bucket**.

Lunchtime

The lunch trolley has arrived on the ward.

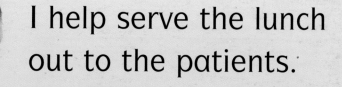

I help serve the lunch out to the patients.

Some children have lunch in bed, but Harry has his at the table.

Today I am meeting Jane for lunch. We choose some sandwiches at the hospital canteen.

Jane works in the Special Care Baby Unit. She looks after very small or **premature** babies. They are kept warm in **incubators**.

Playtime

Most children can get out of bed sometimes.
We have two playrooms for them to play in.

Harry challenges me to a game of pool. I expect
he will win as I am not very good.

Harry has an illness which means he has to visit us regularly. We look at a medical information book together and discuss his condition.

Next I play with Cosmo in the outdoor play area.

Back from theatre

Madeleine has had her operation. I bring her back into her room. She is fast asleep.

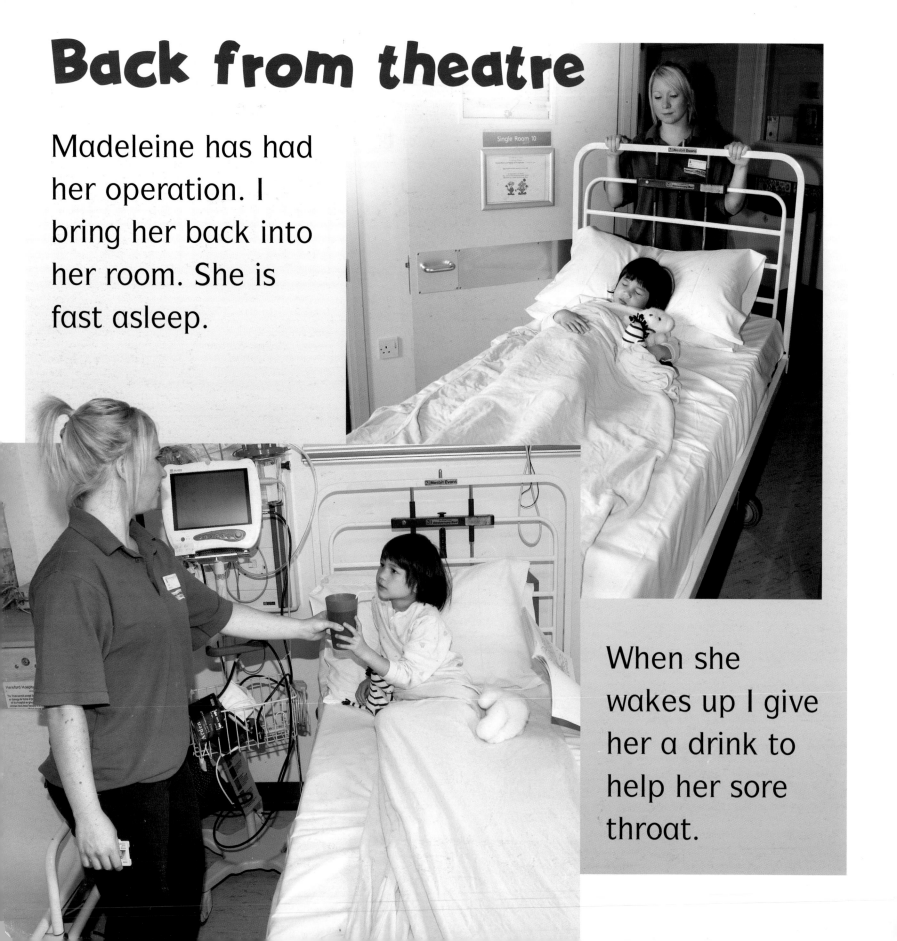

When she wakes up I give her a drink to help her sore throat.

I take her temperature. The electronic thermometer says 36°C so Madeleine's temperature is normal.

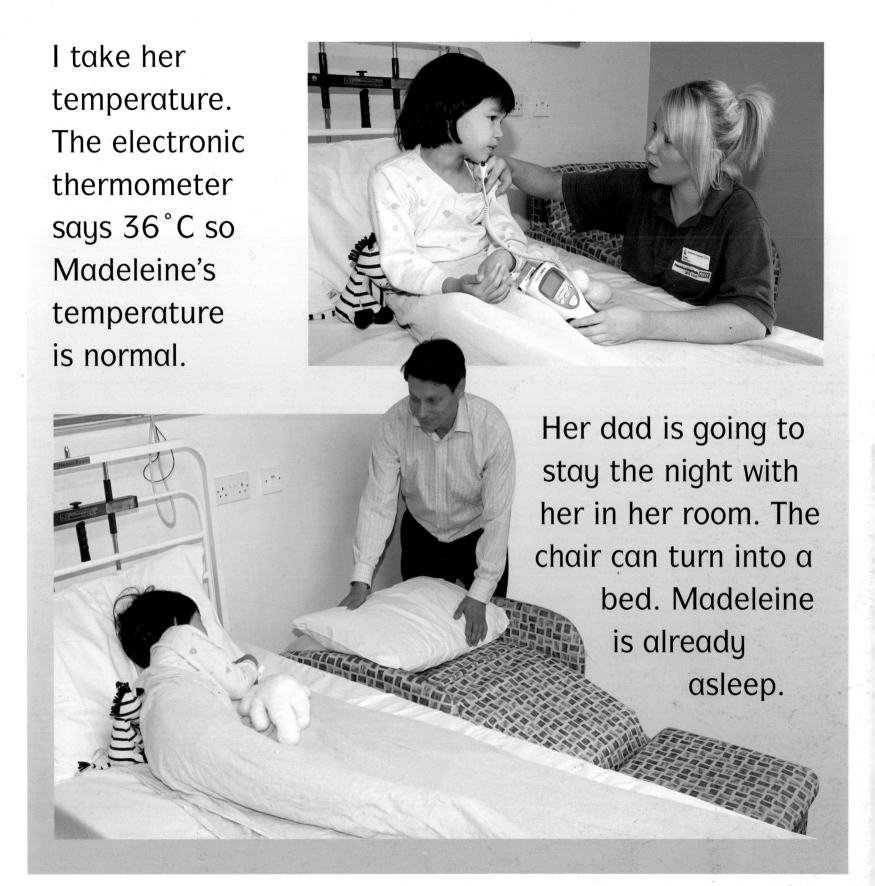

Her dad is going to stay the night with her in her room. The chair can turn into a bed. Madeleine is already asleep.

Updating records

It has been a busy day and it is nearly the end of my shift. I go to the staff kitchen and make myself a cup of tea.

Then I go back to the reception desk. I need to use the computer.

All the information about the patients is on
computer. I fill in the details of how all the
patients are and what treatments they have
had today. It is important to update the
records often.

End of shift

It is now time for me to go home. Before I go, I give the hand-over reports to Ainsley. He is doing a **double shift**.

It has been a good day on the ward. I love being a nurse and helping sick children get better.

Glossary

blood pressure a measurement of how well your blood is pumping around your body

diabetes an illness where the body does not produce enough insulin, making people tired and thirsty

double shift doing two shifts of work, one after the other

glucose a type of sugar in the body

incubator a plastic cot in a hospital that keeps small babies warm and safe

insulin a hormone that controls the level of glucose in your blood

insulin pen a small machine that injects you with insulin

patients people who need to receive treatment from a doctor in a hospital

physiotherapy treating injuries by massaging and exercising the body

premature describes a baby that is born too early

reception the area in a hospital where patients and visitors are welcomed

sharps bucket a bucket where all used sharp objects like needles are put to be destroyed later

shift a part of the day that people take it in turns to work

surgery the process of operating on somebody

theatre the room in a hospital where operations happen

tonsillitis a disease of the tonsils

tonsils two small lumps of tissue at the back of the throat

ward round when a doctor visits all the patients on a ward to see how they are

Index

THE WORLD OF DRAGONS

DRAGON BEHAVIOUR

BY MATT DOEDEN

READING CONSULTANT: BARBARA J. FOX

Rai nited,
a c ng its
re 5LB –

www.raintreepublishers.co.uk
myorders@raintreepublishers.co.uk

First published by Capstone Press © 2013
First published in the United Kingdom in 2013
The moral rights of the proprietor have been asserted

Photo Credits
Capstone: Federico Piatti, 29, Jonathan Mayer, 6–7, 9 (all), 10, 12–13, 18–19, 20–21, 22, 25, Krista Ward & Tod Smith, cover (top & bottom), Richard Pellegrino, 26; Shutterstock: Storozhenko, 4–5, Unholy Vault Designs, cover (background), 1, 14–15, Wampa, 16–17

Design Elements
Shutterstock

Editors: Aaron Sautter & Vaarunika Dharmapala
Designer: Kyle Grenz
Media Researcher: Eric Gohl
Production Specialist: Jennifer Walker

ISBN 978 1 406 26659 7 (paperback)
17 16 15 14 13
10 9 8 7 6 5 4 3 2 1

Printed and bound in China by Leo Paper Products Ltd.

British Library Cataloguing in Publication Data
A full catalogue record for this book is available from the British Library.

CONTENTS

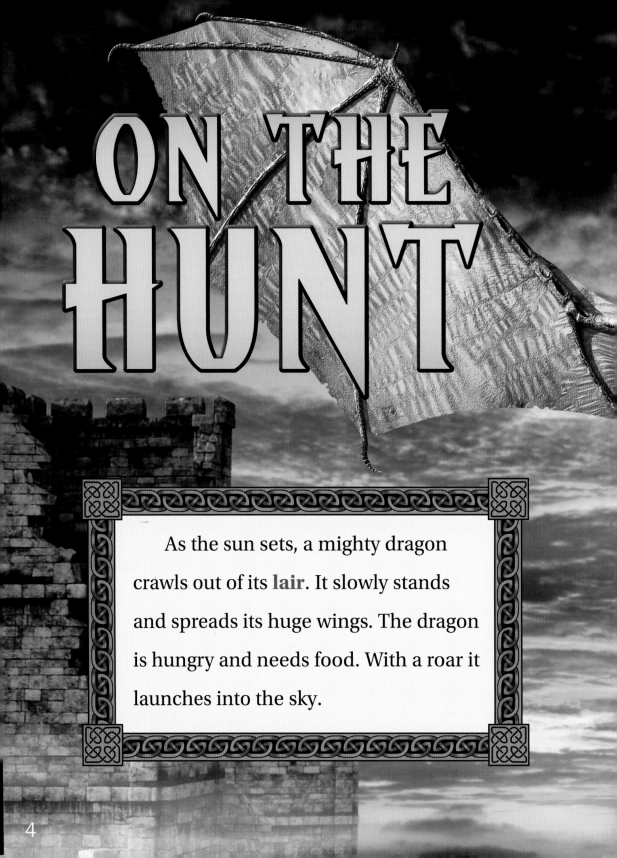

ON THE HUNT

As the sun sets, a mighty dragon crawls out of its **lair**. It slowly stands and spreads its huge wings. The dragon is hungry and needs food. With a roar it launches into the sky.

lair place where a wild animal lives and sleeps

DRAGON FACT

In some stories, dragons cook their meals with their fiery breath.

The dragon soon spots some
sheep. The sheep are easy **prey**. The
dragon snaps one up and swallows
it whole. Then the dragon grabs a
second sheep to take back to its lair.

prey animal hunted by another animal for food

DRAGON LIFE

Dragons have appeared in stories and **myths** for thousands of years. The stories are found all around the world. There are many kinds of dragons in these stories. Most share similar **behaviours**.

myth story told long ago that many people believed to be true

behaviour way an animal or person acts

FLYING DRAGONS

- live mainly in mountain caves or old castles
- often breathe fire, ice, or poison
- usually eat deer, sheep, elk, and other large animals

LAND DRAGONS

- live near swamps, ponds, or streams
- have a poisonous bite
- eat rabbits, squirrels, and other small animals

WATER DRAGONS

- live in underwater caves next to the ocean
- have a poisonous bite
- eat fish, squid, seals, and other sea creatures

Dragons in most stories live in mountain caves. These lairs are often found high up on snowy cliffs. Others live in swamps or deep in the forest.

Dragons' lairs usually have plenty of hunting ground nearby.

Dragons choose their lairs carefully. They need plenty of space to move around. Dragons also sleep for weeks or months at a time. They like to stay safe in secret underground caves.

DRAGON FACT

Some dragons live in old, crumbling castles.

Dragons in most stories have a treasure **hoard**. Dragons believe treasure gives them power. Some dragons collect gold and gems. Others collect magic rings and swords.

hoard large amount of something

Dragons keep their treasure hidden in their lairs.

DRAGON FACT

Powerful adult dragons sometimes eat younger dragons.

Most dragons live alone. They usually come together only to **mate**. If a dragon moves into another dragon's area, watch out. Dragons will often fight to protect their **territories**.

mate to join together to produce young

territory land on which an animal hunts for food

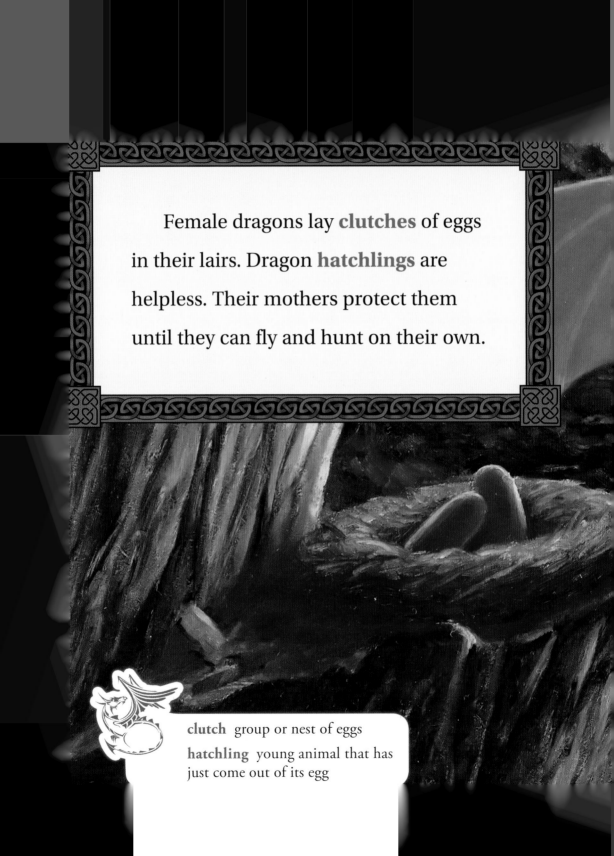

Female dragons lay **clutches** of eggs in their lairs. Dragon **hatchlings** are helpless. Their mothers protect them until they can fly and hunt on their own.

clutch group or nest of eggs
hatchling young animal that has just come out of its egg

DRAGON FACT

In some stories, dragon mothers breathe fire on their eggs to keep them warm.

MIGHTY HUNTERS

Dragons are great hunters. Flying dragons look for food from high in the sky. Others creep through forests to hunt for their meals.

DRAGON FACT

All dragons have excellent eyesight. Flying dragons can spot prey from thousands of metres in the air.

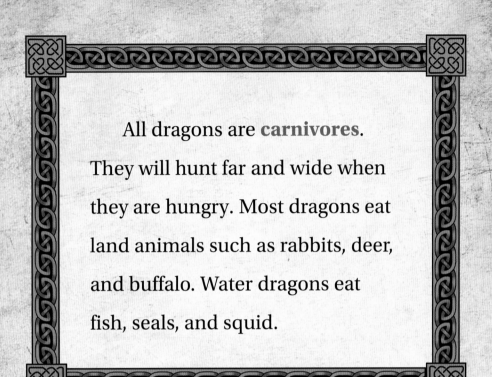

All dragons are **carnivores**. They will hunt far and wide when they are hungry. Most dragons eat land animals such as rabbits, deer, and buffalo. Water dragons eat fish, seals, and squid.

DRAGON FACT

In some stories, big dragons even hunt and eat elephants!

carnivore animal that eats only meat

DRAGONS AND PEOPLE

Dragons and people are enemies in many stories. Dragons sometimes hunt and eat farm animals like cows, sheep, or pigs. Farmers hate it when dragons steal their animals.

DRAGON FACT Some dragons have magical powers. They can control people's thoughts and actions with a single look.

DRAGON FACT

Most dragons love riddles. People sometimes escape from a dragon by telling it a good riddle.

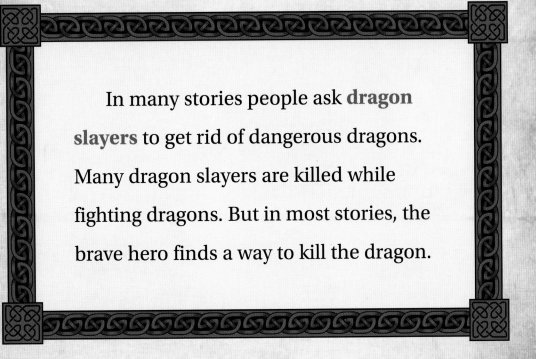

In many stories people ask **dragon slayers** to get rid of dangerous dragons. Many dragon slayers are killed while fighting dragons. But in most stories, the brave hero finds a way to kill the dragon.

dragon slayer someone who specializes in killing dragons

In some stories from Eastern **cultures**, dragons are friendly. They share their knowledge and like to help people. Whether they are fierce or friendly, dragons are amazing mythical creatures.

DRAGON FACT

In rare cases, a dragon might share a close friendship with someone. These dragons may even allow their human friends to ride on them.

culture people's way of life, ideas, customs, and traditions

GLOSSARY

behaviour   way an animal or person acts

carnivore   animal that eats only meat

clutch   group or nest of eggs

culture   people's way of life, ideas, customs, and traditions

dragon slayer   someone who specializes in killing dragons

hatchling   young animal that has just come out of its egg

hoard   large amount of something

lair   place where a wild animal lives and sleeps

mate   to join together to produce young

myth   story told long ago that many people believed to be true

prey   animal hunted by another animal for food

territory   land on which an animal hunts for food and raises its young

Read more

Non-fiction

How to Draw Dragons, Mark Bergin (Bookhouse, 2010)

Fiction

Dragon Rider, Cornelia Funke (Chicken House, 2005)

Dragonblood series, Michael Dahl (Raintree, 2010)

No Such Thing as Dragons, Philip Reeve (Marion Lloyd Books, 2010)

The Hobbit, J.R.R. Tolkien (HarperCollins, 2012)

Websites

FactHound offers a safe, fun way to find websites related to this book. All the sites on FactHound have been researched by our staff.

Here's all you do:

Visit *www.facthound.com*

Type in this code: 9781406266597

INDEX